THE PAINLESS NEGOTIATION

The
Painless
Negotiation

ANCHOR YOUR WAY
TO A GREAT DEAL...
FOR EVERYONE

Steve Thompson

VALUE LIFECYCLE™

THE PAINLESS NEGOTIATION
Anchor Your Way to a Great Deal...for Everyone

ISBN 978-1-5445-2521-1   *Paperback*
978-1-5445-2520-4   *Ebook*

Contents

Foreword

It has been a long and highly competitive sales process, but the key decision makers have assured you that your company is the one they want. Now it's time to meet with procurement. Wasting no time, the procurement manager says, "You may believe you've won the business, but by my evaluation the competition is just as good, technically—maybe even better. They appear faster, and they're certainly cheaper, and if you don't sharpen your pencil, there's no way I can award the business to you and your company."

Does this situation sound familiar? If so, you know exactly how it feels to hear these words.

Your first instinct is to panic. But stop and think about it for a moment. If the competition is truly better, faster, and cheaper, why is procurement wasting their time talking to you? Wouldn't the deal already be awarded to the lowest bidder? You can be sure that the procurement manager is telling your competitors the same thing, and the whole thing may start to feel like a game at this point. But let's be clear, it's a game you can lose dearly if you don't know how to play it—that is, if you aren't prepared to negotiate.

As a seller, you must be comfortable with the certainty that you will always have a competitor who is more desperate to win the business than you. In other words, there will always be a competitor with less qualified sales pipeline who will therefore undercut you by competing on price alone.[1]

But if price were truly the only issue, the salesforce would be obsolete. Buyers could simply add your

---

1 I always wonder about this strategy. After all, this is called selling, not charity. Anyone can give stuff away!

products and services to a "cart" on the internet. We know it's not that simple, and this is exactly what you must bear in mind when procurement tries to make you think it is. Hold your ground (see sidebar)!

There are few words a salesperson hates to hear more than "your price is too high." Yet they are entirely predictable and should be expected for virtually every B2B sale. Why are most sales reps unprepared to respond effectively? This has perplexed me for years. After all, how often do you hear "your price is too low"?

Negotiating effectively begins with selling and positioning effectively to set up the "right negotiation." Then you must have a strategy to manage expected negotiation tactics that procurement will throw at you, such as your price is too high.

One notable aspect of B2B deals is their inherent complexity. There are usually more than one or two items (deal levers) on the table, and you are selling to an outcome facilitated by various products or services (or both), while determining appropriate volumes, discounts, a close date, payment terms, ancillary services, and follow-up support—not to mention terms and conditions, like penalties and warranties.

This complexity is an *advantage* to you in negotiations because it gives you so many options and increased flexibility. As you will see, it is much easier to negotiate a deal with multiple deal levers on the table versus a deal with only one or two items up for discussion. Yet most sales reps fail to take advantage of this "gift" of complexity and are therefore woefully unprepared to interact effectively with procurement. Not only are they unprepared to handle the inevitable *your price is too high* tactic, most times their selling organization can't even tell them what a good deal looks like, much less the minimum they will accept. This is especially true during the final few days of a quarter, when a "good deal" tends to get downgraded to basically "any deal." And that's exactly what they get.

This book addresses an all-too-common challenge sellers present to buyers: not being prepared to negotiate a deal with them and thus delaying the decision to award. In these pages we will explore capturing the value in not just any deal, but a great deal for both you and your customer. This is the fourth volume in the five-part Must-Win Deals Series. The first book, *Must-Win Deals*, reveals the four common things we, as sellers, do to make it challenging for customers to award us key deals. It also explores the idea of pursuing not just any deal, but a great deal. The second book, *The Irresistible Value Proposition*, reveals how to develop a value proposition that gets the customer excited about doing business with you right now! *The Compelling Proposal* then showcases the proposal as a strategic tool to reinforce trust and credibility, making it easier for the customer to choose you (and sell internally), while managing the uncertainty inherent in the real world. The final title, *Can't-Lose Accounts*, delves into delivering the promised value, making renewals simple, referrals enthusiastic, and upselling and cross-selling opportunities much more bountiful. I hope you derive great value from this journey!

It bears repeating that approximately half my work involves training and consulting with procurement specialists, purchasing management, and purchasing executives with some of the largest companies in the world. In these engagements I help them position and negotiate better, more strategic deals with their key suppliers. (As I write these words, I am in Asia helping a buying client position and negotiate critical deals with their top-tier suppliers.) As a result, my viewpoint encompasses more than just the sales side of negotiating, and I want to show you a different perspective from the *other side* of the negotiating table.

So, what is the role of procurement (or purchasing, vendor management, supplier relations, or a host of other euphemisms)? Basically, it is to make you (the seller) cry!

All kidding aside, procurement's role in the buying process is to ensure that their company is getting a good deal from you. As for negotiating, you can be sure that most procurement experts have been to the same one-room school of dealmaking, and they will do everything they can to keep the focus on a single issue—most likely price—to the exclusion of everything else. They also want your company to expend a lot of energy negotiating internally, against yourselves, a subject that gets its own chapter in this book. But it is the very predictability of procurement's single-minded approach to getting their "good deal" that should make preparing for and negotiating with them a routine nonevent in the sales cycle. In spite of this, time and again most selling organizations go to the negotiating table unprepared, reinventing the wheel for every deal.

To be clear, this book isn't about a negotiation *process*. There are ample such processes out there, and some are very good. (I've taught many of them to thousands of buyers and sellers around the globe.)[2]

Instead, what I will share with you is an overarching framework for negotiating, one that directly links

---

2   Like other aspects of sales, I have found that understanding a negotiation process isn't nearly as critical as mastering the fundamental concepts surrounding the negotiation.

how we position a deal before the *formal* negotiation with what we want to accomplish *after* the negotiation. This framework—the Value Lifecycle™—informs how we should sell, propose, negotiate, and then manage accounts after the sale. I have found that companies adept at executing this model increase their conversion rates and shorten their sales cycles. And after the sale they have much less account churn. They also enjoy higher success rates cross-selling and upselling, have higher margins on the deals they close, and keep customers longer. In many cases they are virtually bulletproof from competitor attacks—nobody is going to take their accounts away from them!

Now, let's turn our attention to capturing value by having the "right" negotiation! In this book we will look at negotiating through a strategic lens, but we will also focus on key tactics—the critical things you must act on.

In that spirit let's start by ensuring that we are aiming at the "right" target and are thus ready to negotiate.

CHAPTER 1

Are You Aiming at a Great Deal?

MANAGING THE INTERNAL NEGOTIATION

In the first three books in the Must-Win Deals Series, we focused on how to ensure that you are selling to customer outcomes (making the "right sale"), developing an irresistible value proposition (to get the customer excited about doing business with you), and presenting a compelling proposal with options (to make it easy to buy from you as well as sell internally). In this book you'll learn how these key steps in the

Value Lifecycle™ are integral to the process of setting up the "right negotiation" with the customer. As you'll soon see, you have been negotiating all along.

THE VALUE LIFECYCLE™ IN ONGOING BUSINESS RELATIONSHIPS
Managing Value Throughout the Customer Relationship

Figure 1.1

Figure 1.1 shows where we are in the Value Lifecycle™, capturing value in a great deal for both parties. But let's take a step back and review the steps you've taken to get to that seat at the negotiation table. First, you learned what the customer was trying to accomplish (the outcomes they wanted to achieve) and how they would measure success (so that you knew how they would measure value). You then connected the dots between your products and services and the customer's outcomes to ensure that you were targeting the right deal.

But remember, your goal is not to close just any deal—it's to capture the value you created in a *great deal*. To that end, let's review the three key value questions from the first book in this series, *Must-Win Deals*.

THE THREE KEY VALUE QUESTIONS

In *Must-Win Deals*, we introduced three key value questions. While it may not have been apparent at the time, these questions are the foundation for positioning and then negotiating effectively. Let's review these questions now in the context of the negotiation.

Value Question #1, *Must-Win Deals* (Chapter 4):
Based on the outcomes important to each side, which deal levers would constitute a *great deal* if we were to reach agreement?

Restating an important tenet of outcome-based B2B selling, you *neither sell nor negotiate outcomes*. These are what the customer *buys*. What the customer *pays for* is the right bundle of deal levers that enable your company and the customer to ultimately deliver those outcomes. These deal levers are the moving parts of the negotiation with the customer, so we need to ensure we're negotiating with the right ones. This is the core of the negotiation framework shown in Figure 1.2.

DEVELOPING A VALUE NEGOTIATION FRAMEWORK

#1 Based on the Outcomes important to each side, what Deal Levers would constitute a **Great Deal** if we were to reach agreement?

Figure 1.2

Note that both sides will come into a potential sale and the subsequent negotiation with deal levers that are important to them. In many cases, there are some deal levers that *both sides agree upon* and want in the deal, and these naturally create joint value. Typically, these deal levers are easy to negotiate as neither side wants to leave them out of the deal. The remaining deal levers—the ones where both sides may disagree on, say, the value of the item or its timing—are what make up the bulk of the negotiation. That is the focus of this book.

> Value Question #2, *The Irresistible Value Proposition* (Chapter 1): Based on desired outcomes, what are the impacts of the most likely alternative (MLA) each side must accept if there is no agreement?

Understanding the potential value you can create for your customer begins with determining the alternative you are being compared to. That's why as a seller, the second way you should look at any potential opportunity is to say *no deal is going to happen,* then determine the most likely alternative each side must accept. I realize this sounds self-defeating—after all, we are paid to win deals—but to truly understand the selling situation and the dynamics of the negotiation, you must evaluate what happens to each side if there is *no deal,* as shown in Figure 1.3.

DEVELOPING A VALUE NEGOTIATION FRAMEWORK

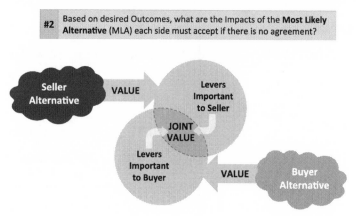

#2 Based on desired Outcomes, what are the Impacts of the **Most Likely Alternative** (MLA) each side must accept if there is no agreement?

Figure 1.3

Analyzing the customer's alternative shows you what you are selling and negotiating against. When you understand how painful each side's alternative is, you can determine how compelling a deal is. Simply put, the more painful the alternative, the more compelling the deal. However, there are several other critical insights we gain by analyzing each side's alternative that will greatly impact the negotiation, and we'll discuss these shortly.

Value Question #3, *The Painless Negotiation* (Chapter 2): Based on desired outcomes, what anchors must we manage, and how should we anchor?

We will explore this final value question in detail in Chapter 2. As you'll see, anchors will have the greatest impact on how the value you create will ultimately be divided. You will also see how you have been anchoring the sale and negotiation from the very beginning! But before we get into the negotiation with the customer, let's discuss an important topic concerning the preparation for negotiations, the *internal negotiation*— that is, the one within your own company.

THE INTERNAL NEGOTIATION

I have long contended that not enough attention is given to the internal negotiation, the one where you work out with the appropriate stakeholders within your company the specific deal levers you should bring to the negotiation table along with the priorities and limits of each of those levers. Instead, sellers' internal negotiations almost always *get in the way* of the external negotiation. They usually take place near the end of a sales cycle, often in a reactive and panic-filled atmosphere, and as a result they tend to be contentious, challenging, and counterproductive to closing a great deal. This is precisely what savvy procurement professionals are counting on. They want you to spend time and energy negotiating against your own company, leaving little time and energy for negotiation with them.

What is the internal negotiation really about? To answer that question, let's go back to the first value question: "Based on the outcomes important to each side, which deal levers would constitute a *great deal* if we were to reach agreement?" As a quick review, a great deal accomplishes the following:

→ It brings high value to the customer because it meets their buying objectives and supports their desired outcomes.

→ It brings high value to you, the seller, because it meets your sales objectives and supports your account/business strategy.

→ It contains the key deal levers that allow both sides to ultimately *deliver the outcomes and value.*

Figure 1.4 provides a template for listing and prioritizing deal levers to help you build a great deal.

DETERMINING A GREAT DEAL

Based on the Outcomes each side is trying to achieve, determine a **Great Deal:**

- List all Deal Levers
- Ranking or Priority
- Limit (Ask for – Accept)

Levers	Limits
1._____	(Ask – Accept)
2._____	(Ask – Accept)
3._____	(Ask – Accept)
4._____	(Ask – Accept)
5._____	(Ask – Accept)
6._____	(Ask – Accept)

Figure 1.4

Determining a great deal begins with three straightforward steps. First, based on the outcomes important to both sides, make a list of the deal levers that should be in the deal. Next, because not every lever is of equal importance in a given deal, prioritize those deal levers. Start by considering higher-priority levers that must stay in the deal for you to achieve your sales goal. Then identify the lower-priority levers you would be willing to trade away to obtain something of greater value. This is how most successful business deals are negotiated, but it only works if you have carefully considered and prioritized all the levers in the deal. Failing that, you will not be prepared to trade effectively.

Finally, world-class organizations deliberately involve internal stakeholders early in the sales cycle to collaboratively define clear upper and lower *limits* for each lever. You can think of a limit as a kind of "guardrail," a barrier designed to keep each lever "in its lane," preventing you from trading away too much of any given item. For example:

→ Discount: Offer 25%, but if pressed we'll go up to 35%.

→ Quantity: Ask for an initial order of 1,500 units. If the customer objects, we will take a minimum volume of 1,000.

→ Close: August 31 preferred close. If the client delays, we will honor the remaining portions of the deal only until September 30.

Sit down with your internal stakeholders as early in the sales cycle as possible and determine the limits on all your deal levers. You can always revise the values as the deal evolves and new information becomes available. This is the essence of your *internal negotiation*—sorting out what you and your company really want (or need) and what you're willing to accept well before the heightened emotions and tensions of the formal negotiation at the end of a sales campaign. If you do not conduct your internal negotiation this way, it will almost certainly conflict with the external negotiation with the customer, usually in an atmosphere of panic at the end of the sales cycle (likely at the end of a quarter)—something I see all too often.

What's more, a key mark of world-class organizations is that they empower their sales reps to negotiate any deal, provided the deal levers are within internally agreed limits. Eliminating the start-stop cadence of tactical negotiating, with the inevitable harried calls or flights back to HQ for permission, can *significantly* compress the time needed to negotiate and close deals. It also drives up the quality of those deals, which is good for the sales rep, good for the business, and good for the customer—a rare triple win!

Defining deal levers and limits ahead of time gives everyone a clear view of the target they are trying to hit, preparing your selling organization to negotiate the *right way* in pursuit of a great deal. Conversely, if you have failed to work with internal stakeholders to establish clear levers and limits, then what will you be prepared to accept? In my experience, sales organizations (especially those without enough sales pipeline) will take just about anything. When you aim low, where do you expect to hit? Whatever your answer, think even lower—right about foot level!

In roughly three out of four engagements, the selling organizations I work with don't know what a great deal looks like based on the outcomes important to each side. For their part, the buying organizations that hire me virtually never know what a great deal looks like. Taken together, it's a wonder deals ever get done—much less great deals for each side!

So, how much value could you bring your organization if you always aimed for and crafted a great deal? And how much value could you bring your customers if you took the time early in the sales cycle to educate them on the key elements of a great deal based on their desired outcomes? In each case you would bring significant value while making your company stand out from the buyer's alternative, helping them make an informed decision to buy from you.

When we fail to gain internal alignment and educate our customer about what a great deal looks like, we set in motion a process that will almost assuredly result in a panicked and chaotic negotiation at the end of the sales cycle—a negotiation both with ourselves and with an uninformed customer. These sales rarely end well for either party.

DETERMINE THE NEGOTIATION STRUCTURE AND POWER

Much has been written about B2B negotiations. But in most books, articles, and other publications I've read, the negotiation is treated as a discrete "event"— one that occurs *near the end* of the sales cycle. In this book, I hope to show you that effective negotiating is anything but that. It is an ongoing process that you set in motion at your very first customer meeting. Sellers who understand and implement this start-to-finish principle of negotiating are much more successful at closing great deals. They embrace negotiating at every stage, from planning through procurement. In other words, they are never not negotiating!

To understand the underlying structure of any negotiation, let's turn our attention back to the second value question: "Based on desired outcomes, what are the impacts of the *most likely alternative* (MLA) each side must accept if there is no agreement?" To answer, you must analyze the alternative you are competing against and ensure that your customer understands that alternative. This is important because your increment of value over the alternative represents your value to the customer, and it will enable you to put more value on the table than the alternative, helping you win the deal.

The second value question continues to build our negotiation framework, as shown in Figure 1.5.

DEVELOPING A VALUE NEGOTIATION FRAMEWORK

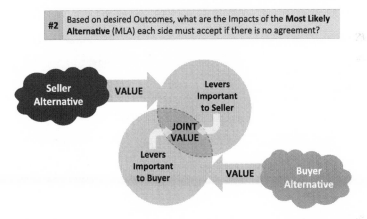

Figure 1.5

Each side's alternative provides the underlying structure and frames the negotiation because neither buyer nor seller would rationally accept a deal worse than their alternative. If a deal is to happen, it must end up somewhere between these alternatives. This is the territory of a win-win deal.

One of the most important dynamics of negotiating is the *perception* of power. The factors that will have a significant impact on the final deal negotiated are 1) which side has power (and how much), 2) how that power was obtained, and 3) how that power affects the behavior of the parties—during the sale and the formal negotiation. By evaluating the *impacts* to each alternative based on the outcomes important to each side, you can determine how good or how bad each side's alternative is. Then, comparing each side's alternative should reveal the party that can walk away from a deal with the least pain. This is the party with the power in the negotiation.

What does this mean in a practical sense when it comes to negotiating? If you determine that the customer has the power (because their alternative is better than yours), then you're not likely to get everything you want out of the deal, and you should determine what you *must get* for the deal to work for you. This is why it is so important to determine what a great deal looks like ahead of time and prioritize your deal levers accordingly. If you determine that you have the power in the negotiation, then you should expect to get most (if not all) of what you want in the deal, and you should not have to trade away much value.

The most common situation I encounter in the real world is that both sides have fairly ugly (painful) alternatives. When this is the case, power is not the issue (neither side has any), and both sides should work hard to craft a deal.

You can't understand the underlying structure and dynamics of any sale or negotiation if you don't first understand each side's alternative to doing a deal, which tells you who has the power.

It's important to note, though, that power is neither absolute nor static. It will shift throughout a sales cycle. As an example, after you present options to your customer and allow them to help construct the right deal for them, it becomes *their deal.* But, perhaps counterintuitively, this *increases* your power, because they are now invested in getting that deal closed. Or perhaps after a lengthy evaluation, your organization is selected as the vendor of choice. Your power is now increased because of the political implications for procurement if they are not able to close a deal with you.

INCREASING YOUR POWER

You might protest at this point that this is all a lot easier to embrace (and execute) when you have the power in the negotiation. And you are right! Remember, power is a function of each side's alternative, which gives you two key tools to increase your power in the sale and the subsequent negotiation. First, you can improve your alternative. This usually means ensuring that you have a robust qualified sales pipeline so that no single deal will hurt you because you have plenty of options for meeting or exceeding your quota. In other words, you can say *no* and walk away from a bad deal!

The second way to increase your power is to make your customer's alternative worse. How do you accomplish that? By making your solution so valuable to the customer that they won't seriously consider another alternative.[3] How much easier will your negotiation be when you've sold significant value to your customer *and* you have a full sales pipeline? Strong pipelines are like *backbones*—giving salespeople the ability to stand tall and just say *no*. However, a nicer way to say "no" is to *trade* for something you want in return, which we'll explore in Chapter 4.

Now, let's look at how the value you've worked so hard to create will ultimately be divided.

---

3   You should be using both of these tools every day, constantly striving to improve your alternative while making your customer's alternative worse!

CHAPTER 2

Preparing for the "Right Negotiation"

IT'S ALL ABOUT EFFECTIVE ANCHORING

What if you have not taken all the steps described in the previous chapter? Or maybe you have, but haven't done them all that well, and now you face a tough negotiation with procurement?

You could just call me. After all, this is often the point in the sale where clients get me involved.[4] The classic

---

4   For some reason, I never seem to get a call when deals are going well!

scenario goes like this: the sales campaign has gone on for months, they've reached the formal negotiation, and the deal is stuck. Sales management and the account team are anxious to bring the deal in before the end of the quarter (hard to believe, right?), and things appear to be at an impasse with procurement. When I ask sales management what the trouble is, invariably I hear, "We have a negotiation problem," and they need help getting the deal unstuck. Why do they believe it's a negotiation issue? "Because procurement is killing us on price and threatening to push the award to next quarter or, worse, award the business to a competitor."

After the first few dozen times going through this, I realized that the real culprit was not the formal negotiation, which at best was a distant, secondary issue. The negotiation simply served as a pressure point that exposed all the sins and peccadillos—the shortcuts, wishful thinking, unpreparedness, poor communication, etc.—that marked the sales cycle up to that point. Over time, I was able to sort these problems into two broad categories: 1) not *selling* value and 2) not *delivering* value for previous purchases.

In our classic scenario, the account team has failed to sell to the customer's outcomes (they haven't connected the dots between the customer's outcomes and the right deal levers), and they lack a relevant or interesting value proposition. As a result, they are *not creating value for the customer* when selling, and they have set the stage for the wrong negotiation. This is what procurement lives for, and their typical response is to make the negotiation all about price, giving the selling organization little recourse but to offer discounts and giveaways to close the deal before the end of the quarter.

Thankfully, there's a happy alternative to this all-too-familiar drama—one that handily flips the script. Procurement's greatest fear is that a seller, following the concepts in the Value Lifecycle™, has sold *value* to someone that matters in their organization. That value must be delivered within a certain time frame, which means that the *deal must close by a certain date*. Now, price and threats of delay are no longer procurement's "nuclear option."

The second broad problem category, not *delivering* value for previous purchases, logically occurs when the account team is selling to a customer who has already bought from their company. These are often long-term buyers, and while the seller may know what they've previously sold, they have no idea of the *value they have delivered* to their customer. In these cases, it's safe to say that the customer also doesn't clearly know the past value they've received. Why is this a problem? Because in this vacuum of ignorance, the buyer's assumption will almost certainly be that they have spent too much, and they will be hell-bent on getting a better deal using the only metric that makes sense in the absence of value: price (meaning lower price or higher discount).

In short, not creating value when selling and/or failing to ensure value delivery from previous purchases (when selling to an existing customer) are the primary reasons that deals get stuck at the point of negotiation.

We'll discuss past value delivered (PVD) in more detail in the fifth book of the Must-Win Deals Series, **Can't-Lose Accounts.**

Let's summarize the key things that ensure we are setting up the right negotiation. These are the clear boxes we should have checked prior to what is commonly viewed as the formal negotiation.

→ Sell to customer outcomes and present a compelling value proposition.

→ Validate with the customer the key deal levers required to produce those outcomes.

→ Present the customer with options, allowing them to buy from you and effectively construct the right deal—making it *their deal*.

→ If the buyer is an existing customer, ensure you have delivered the promised value from previous purchases and received credit for that value.

Each of these items serves to anchor the sale and subsequent negotiation, which brings us to our third value question: "Based on desired outcomes, what anchors must we manage, and how should we anchor?"

WHAT IS AN ANCHOR?

The concept of anchoring can be a little tricky to describe, but it's easy if we set our metaphorical anchor aside for a moment and imagine ourselves on an "actual" fishing boat. You might think of an anchor as something that pins you firmly in one place, but as any angler will tell you, when you drop an anchor from a boat, the boat will then drift in an arc around the drop point.[5] So when you put an anchor down, in effect you're saying, *Let's see what we can catch in this general area.* This is what happens in negotiations. When an anchor is effectively "dropped," the final negotiated deal you "catch" will generally stay close to the anchor point.

When you anchor, you are changing the frame of reference (drop point) of the sale and negotiation, so you should always anchor thoughtfully and strategically, as what you start selling is usually what you end up

---

5   The amount of drift will depend, of course, on the amount of slack in the line, so for the sake of simplicity let's just call it "medium" slack.

negotiating. (Think about it: it's much easier to drop an anchor than to reel it back in.) It is also important not to overtly or immediately react to the other side's anchors. As soon as you do, they control the conversation, and you are effectively helping them "catch their own fish." Figure 2.1 illustrates how buyers and sellers routinely anchor.

WHAT ARE EXAMPLES OF ANCHORS?

- How do Buyers anchor sales and negotiations?
  - Your price is 20% too high...
  - Your competition is including that service for free...
  - Our budget is only "X"...
  - RFPs and RFQs
- How do Sellers anchor sales and negotiations?
  - "What" they start selling
  - How they position and propose it
  - Previous deals

Figure 2.1

Now, let's look at how buyers will typically try to anchor you—and how you're likely to respond.

"Your Price is 20 Percent Too High."

When you hear these words, what happens? You forget everything else, focus only on price, and measure your negotiating success from that point forward by how much you can get the buyer to come off that 20 percent number. What is the buyer doing here? They're dropping a big, fat price anchor, and they can now relax while you and your sales team bust out your fishing poles, ready to make *their* catch! In reality, they'd probably settle for 10 percent, but the final deal is likely to be a lot closer to twenty because every increment down from that number will make you feel more and more like an expert negotiator.

"Our Budget Is Only 'X'"

This classic buyer anchor is designed to make you forget about everything else you are trying to accomplish and focus only on "X." If you have ever tried to cram a million-dollar solution into a half-million-dollar budget, you know this well (it happens all too often). Of course, this is akin to the discount anchor, and similar seller behaviors apply.

Requests for "Compliance"

Perhaps the biggest anchors that buyers use are RFPs and RFQs. These documents are the buyer's way of telling you *what* you get to talk about, *how* you can talk about it, and *when*, completely framing and anchoring the conversation. *This is why so many deals are won or lost before the RFP stage is even complete.* (Just imagine if you were asked to help write the specs for an RFP. You'd jump at the chance, of course, because you'd now have the opportunity to anchor the deal in your favor.)

As sellers we often do a big part of the buyer's work by inadvertently anchoring ourselves. For instance, if we begin a selling motion talking about a product or service, why should we be surprised when the negotiation is only about the "price" of that product or service? That's how we set it up, and we can hardly blame the buyer for taking advantage of our mistake!

Discounted Past

Finally, one of the most difficult anchors to deal with is another one that we create—or sometimes our company does. Have you ever taken over an account where the previous sales rep did some "unnatural acts" to bring a deal in before quarter or year-end? If so, you can be sure that the starting point for any new negotiation will be the concessions the customer received last time—and they *will* want more! Perhaps no situation better illustrates the need to anchor and negotiate effectively than past deals done with a customer.

As you can see, anchors are powerful and effective negotiating tools. But they only work against you if you don't recognize them for what they are and respond (or not) accordingly.

HOW TO MANAGE ANCHORS

Anchors are one of the most common tools employed by procurement professionals, so it's critical that you know how to effectively manage them. Note that you are *managing* (versus *avoiding* or *neutralizing*) because you cannot control the behavior of the other party in a negotiation. However, you can be sure that in any negotiation where you don't control your behavior, you will be anchored!

Let's assume that procurement just told you, "The competition is 20 percent cheaper." There are three simple steps to managing this anchor:

1. Deflect (do not react by countering, defending, or arguing)

   "So, what I hear you saying is that you want us to reduce our price..."

2. Re-anchor on the bundle of deal levers that support the desired outcomes

   "As you'll recall, the price is related to all of these items in our offer required to produce the outcomes important to you; therefore..."

3. Start trading—don't concede on a single deal lever

   "There might be a path for at least getting some price reduction; however, here are the impacts to the outcomes, and this is what we will require in return..."

What "deflect" really means here is that you are "ignoring" or sidestepping the intended impact of their anchor by repeating it (20 percent cheaper) back to them—with a twist. An all-too-common tactic used by procurement is to try and force a single-issue negotiation. But the problem with negotiating a single issue is mathematical: one side can only win if the other loses, an arrangement they want you to agree to *on their terms*. But you're not going to play that game. In this context, *deflect* simply means not legitimizing their anchor by countering, defending, or arguing. By responding to their "competition is 20 percent cheaper" anchor with, "What I hear you saying is that you want us to reduce our price," you not only avoid repeating their anchor and legitimizing the competitive "bogeyman," you also force them to agree that the real issue is that they simply want to pay you less.

Of course, you should follow this up by re-anchoring the conversation on the outcomes important to the customer and the bundle of deal levers required to deliver those outcomes. If you have sold to your customer's outcomes and then educated them on the appropriate level of products and services needed to achieve those outcomes, then you have set the stage for re-anchoring the negotiation on what the customer wants to achieve. Your response then might be, *"Remember, the price is related to all of the deal levers in our offer that are required to produce the outcomes that you have said are important to you. Therefore..."* Don't allow the conversation to focus on any single item or lever in your offer.

Finally, as you'll learn in Chapter 3, do not concede on any deal lever (including price). Rather, trade for items that are important to you. This is the essence of not just managing anchors but of negotiating effectively. For example, *"There might be a path for at least getting some price reduction, but here's how that would impact the outcomes, and in return we'll require..."*

Despite the one-note tactics typically used by procurement professionals, anchoring is a great tool for shaping a non-zero-sum negotiation—one that can result in a *great deal* for both sides. So how do you use anchors to your advantage? (After all, your goal is not to "play defense" through the entire sale and negotiation!)

HOW (AND WHEN, AND WHAT) TO ANCHOR

The good news is that anchors work both ways, and if you have effectively anchored your value in the key activities leading up to the negotiation, you've set the stage for driving a final deal more to your liking. What does that look like? From the very first meeting, you focused on the customer's outcomes, connecting those outcomes to the right deal levers needed to produce them. You then developed an irresistible value proposition that was all about the outcomes important to the customer and the incremental value you would provide. Finally, you presented options in your proposal, each representing different outcomes (and value) to the customer, allowing them to help shape the deal.

All along, you've been *anchoring the sale and the negotiation*,[6] and if you've done this well, your customer will now be playing the "right game," one governed by the outcomes important to them and directly linked to your strategic goals in the sale. In short, the extent to which you

6　This is what it means to be "negotiating all the time."

have anchored the negotiation by attaching your unique value to the customer's desired outcomes is the extent to which you will be inoculated against their price anchors.

Now that you know what anchors are, let's complete our negotiation framework in Figure 2.2.

HOW SHOULD WE ANCHOR EFFECTIVELY?

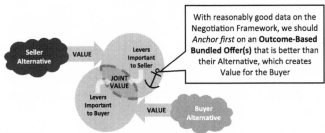

Figure 2.2

Note that your objective is to anchor on a bundled offer that is better than your customer's alternative. This immediately highlights the incremental value for your customer and *gets their attention*. Unfortunately, concepts and models don't always conform to the world we live in, which is complex, uncertain, and always changing. For example, perhaps you have not anchored effectively up to this point in the sales process because of all the uncertainty surrounding a number of the key decision makers for your opportunity. If this is the case, all is not lost. You can regain control of the sale and negotiation by pulling it all together in a compelling proposal, one built around your customer's desired outcomes. Your proposal should feature three bundled offers (multiple acceptable options) with the expectation that at least one will prove more valuable than the customer's alternative. This allows your customer to participate in building the best deal for themselves—making it in a sense "their deal." This will enable you to manage that uncertainty, re-anchor the sale and negotiation, and regain a large measure of control. Look again at the outline of the proposal in Figure 2.3.

MANAGING UNCERTAINTY AND PROPOSING OUTCOMES
Compelling Proposal Presentation Template

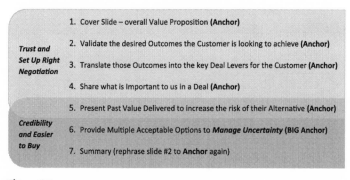

Figure 2.3

In effect, your seven-part proposal is a series of anchors that reframe what you want to be talking about, how you will talk about it, and ultimately what you will end up negotiating. One key objective of the compelling proposal is to set up the right negotiation. Multiple acceptable options are both the "heart" of the proposal as well as the biggest anchor. Figure 2.4 illustrates how these options fit into our negotiation framework.

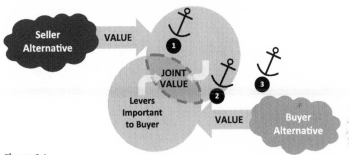

MANAGING UNCERTAINTY
The Power of Multiple Acceptable Options

- Important to Each Side (Great Deal)
- Each Side's Alternative
- Anchor on Multiple Acceptable Options

Figure 2.4

In Figure 2.4, anchors one, two, and three represent the three multiple acceptable options you might present to the customer. In this case, your customer would feel that the third option is no better than their alternative and immediately focus on options one and two, each of which creates value for them. Better still, options one and two increase your odds of winning as you are now competing against yourself!

Thus far we've covered the concept of a great deal to ensure you are aiming at the right target for your opportunity—and that you're ready to negotiate. We've also reviewed the power of anchoring in setting up the right negotiation. But before we look at how to negotiate the *right way*, let's turn our attention back to the case story. How are Paul and the Agile account team handling the internal negotiation (by defining a great deal)? And are they anchoring the right negotiation with MFS?

CASE STORY CONTINUED

Cast of Characters – Recap

1. *Paul Stockard: Agile Sales Rep*: Paul is the Sales Rep for Agile Information Solutions (Agile), and has been calling on Worldwide Financial Solutions,

Inc. (Worldwide) for the past five months. Today, Worldwide is in the process of being acquired by Mega Financial Services (MFS) creating potentially the largest opportunity Agile has ever pursued.

2. *Jane Jones: Agile Sales Engineer:* Jane handles all the technical aspects of an opportunity and manages proof-of-concept tests with a customer prior to a sale. She also supports the customer after the sale.

3. *Douglas Hand: Agile Lead Engineer for Services and Support:* Doug is responsible for implementation after the sale, as well as customer support. If Agile is chosen, he and his team will lead the integration project.

4. *Jared Carlisle: Agile Senior Financial Analyst:* Jared's job is to ensure that any Agile offering will be profitable to the company as well as in line with deals given to other customers. He also helps account teams quantify the value they expect to deliver to customers.

5. *Tim Rosser: Agile VP of Sales:* Tim is an experienced IT sales executive who is known to be unflappable, as well as a great coach and

mentor. Paul and his team have a very good relationship with Tim.

6. ***Caroline Borders:*** *Agile VP of Legal:* Caroline is an experienced attorney who is savvy in the technology space and handles most legal negotiations of contracts, terms, and conditions with customers.

7. ***Susan Renly:*** *Worldwide Chief Information Officer (CIO):* Susan has been a long-time supporter of Agile and Paul. The recent acquisition of Worldwide by MFS has created a terrific career opportunity for her as she is in the running for the position of CIO of MFS. (The current CIO recently left the company.) This would be a significant jump in responsibility and pay, and seems contingent on Agile winning the business and the successful integration of Worldwide into MFS.

8. ***Bill Sellers:*** *MFS SVP of Operations:* Bill heads up the Steering Committee and has been charged by the MFS board of directors with completing the Worldwide IT integration in less than four months. It appears he has been given significant incentives to do so, as he is anxious to get this

integration underway. Bill was instrumental in selecting Agile.

9. ***Jack Grossman:*** *MFS VP of Technology:* Also on the steering committee, Jack's role is to determine the technical merits of the integration approach. He is also in the running for the newly open MFS CIO position. Jack is a big supporter of JCN, the primary competition for the opportunity, and has proven to not be an advocate for Agile or their approach.

10. ***Stephanie Holder:*** *MFS Sr. Procurement Manager:* MFS has a reputation as a very tough negotiator and Stephanie is a big reason for that. It also appears that the Procurement Department wields a lot of influence and power at MFS. Paul and Stephanie are about to enter into a critical negotiation.

When Paul and the account team learned that JCN was offering to do the Worldwide integration by giving away their competing software and services—absolutely free—it was hardly good news, but it confirmed that MFS's clear alternative was JCN. As a result, Paul and his team took a big step back and analyzed the alternative that Agile was competing against. They knew that they couldn't afford to fall into the trap of competing head-to-head with JCN on their terms. They needed to carefully qualify the opportunity for Agile and, if it passed muster, determine how they were going to win it.

Sixteen million in savings out of the box would be a strong opener for JCN, but the savings would be more than offset by the cost of their proprietary hardware. What's more, their installation timeline—at least two months beyond the board's deadline—would be a big negative. MFS, after all, would have to consider the cost, both in stock value and reputation, of missing market expectations in the event of a delayed integration, with implications that would go all the way to the CEO. Paul was betting that Bill Sellers would not risk choosing a vendor that would almost certainly go over the all-important deadline, and he knew that Bill had been given strong incentives to ensure that didn't happen!

But despite all the tangible and intangible costs and risks of choosing JCN for this project, MFS would think long and hard before putting their long-term relationship with such a strategically important supplier at risk. For their part, JCN was already playing hardball. Behind the scenes they had succeeded in convincing MFS's CEO to move the presentation date up, and now Paul and the team had fewer than three days to prepare Agile's proposal presentation for the steering committee. To make matters worse, MFS had just announced that they were acquiring American Investment Corporation (AIC), a niche player who completely outsourced their IT operations to JCN.

In a productive meeting with Bill Sellers and Susan Renly, Paul had validated the outcomes that were important to MFS. He left the meeting certain that Susan was a strong supporter and sponsor of Agile, and he had begun to believe that Bill was leaning Agile's way. He and the team had done their homework, and with Susan's help, his value proposition crisply answered why Bill and MFS should care. It also clearly laid out Agile's incremental value and exactly what they would deliver.

Of course, the answer to the question *why now?* could not have been more obvious: time was of the essence, and only Agile could bring a successful solution to bear within the board's time frame. Everything would hinge on the compelling proposal the Agile team would present and how good Paul and his team made Bill look to the board and CEO.

The proposal presentation had gone as well as could be expected, especially because of the preparation of Paul and his team and their refusal to be anchored by JCN's offer of "free software and services." Instead, Paul and the Agile team re-anchored the proposal on meeting or exceeding the board's timeline. Despite a few theatrics and attempts to sidetrack Paul's presentation (mostly by Jack Grossman), they were formally selected as vendor of choice by the Steering Committee late last Friday. It was Bill Sellers who called Paul with the news. Now Paul and his team must prepare for what is shaping up to be a tough negotiation tomorrow with Stephanie Holder. Today, he is meeting again with the key Agile internal stakeholders to finalize a great deal and develop their negotiation strategy.

* * *

The meeting convened at 8:00 a.m. Monday morning. Paul was there, along with Tim, Jared, Doug, and Caroline. After congratulations from everyone for winning this critical business, Paul spent the first half hour briefing Caroline and Jared on the results of the proposal presentation the previous Friday. Other than a few clarifying questions, the meeting went smoothly.

Tim asked Caroline for the status of resolving the legal terms and conditions with MFS, and she was happy to report that Susan Renly had really come through in expediting the Agile master contract. Everything was on track to be completed by tomorrow. This brought a guarded smile from Tim. His long tenure in the sales world had taught him that nothing is real until the contract is signed.

Tim then asked Paul for the status of the final written proposal that was due at MFS that morning. Paul glanced at his watch and said that Jane Jones should be delivering it to MFS at that very moment. This coaxed another smile and a nod from Tim, who quickly brought the team around to the task at hand, revising and finalizing what a great deal looked like for Agile and MFS. Paul passed around the account team's notes from Friday's proposal presentation. He then went to the whiteboard and put up the original great deal analysis that was developed before the presentation (see Table 2.1). This would be the starting point of the discussions today.

The most notable changes would result from MFS choosing a slightly modified version of Option #3, which included both the AIC and future acquisitions for (hopefully) a three-year period.

Preliminary Great Deal for Agile and MFS

Priority	Levers	Limits
1.	WFSI Software Discount ~$14M	30% Discount – 35% Discount
2.	Implementation Services $920K	$950K – $800K
3.	Training 10 MFS Staff Onsite $80K	$80K Onsite – $60K Offsite
4.	Close Deal in 4 Weeks	2 Weeks – 4 Weeks / Schedule Slip
5.	Platinum Support $240K	$250K – $125K / Gold Level
6.	Payment Terms (Up front)	Up front – ½ Up front / ½ Completion
7.	Case Study and References	Case Study and References – Reference Only
8.	CVR Quarterly with SVP and CIO	Quarterly – Semiannually

Ag*i*le

Table 2.1

Throughout the meeting, Paul's cell phone buzzed every ten minutes or so. He didn't want to interrupt the flow of the meeting since everyone was there to discuss his deal (and he was the most junior attendee), but Paul had a feeling that the calls had something to do with MFS. During a break, he checked his messages, six calls: two from Susan Renly and four from Jane Jones, the account sales engineer.

Both Susan and Jane urged him to return their calls as soon as possible, but Jane was starting to sound frantic. He immediately phoned Susan, only to get her voicemail. He asked her to call back as soon after 11:00 a.m. as possible. Checking his email, a new message from Stephanie Holder stated that she was scheduling their negotiation meeting for 9:00 a.m. tomorrow and that she expected Tim Rosser to also attend as she wanted someone there from Agile who had the authority to make a decision.

Just what I need right now, Paul fretted. *She's already started the power games before we're even at the table.* He forwarded the email to Tim, then called Jane. What she said left him reeling.

"Paul, Susan was trying to reach you about an hour ago," Jane began, her voice tinged with frustration. "When she couldn't get you, she cornered me when I was delivering the proposal to MFS. Susan discovered that JCN has just brought in a revised proposal that features a *brand-new cloud-based offering* they have supposedly been developing!"

"Oh, for the love of..." Paul exclaimed. "I mean, I guess I shouldn't be surprised, but *come on!*"

"But wait, there's more!" Jane said, aping the tone of a bad infomercial. "The pricing for their revised proposal is essentially *free for the first year*, with JCN covering all integration costs. Now the rest of the account team is freaking out because no one has any information about JCN's cloud-based offering!"

"What do you want to bet that's because until this weekend there was no such animal?" Paul swallowed hard, then asked Jane to let Susan know he would be in his current meeting for at least a couple more hours and would call her back as soon as he could. "Jane," he added, almost as an afterthought, "in the meantime, when you get back to Susan, ask her for *any other information* she may have about JCN's new offering. Something about this doesn't smell right, and we're going to need all the clues we can get to find the source of the odor!"

Satisfied there was nothing else to be done for the moment, Paul returned to the meeting and asked Tim to check his email for the message from the senior procurement manager at MFS. He then shared with the attendees the news about JCN's bombshell proposal. In response to the flurry of questions that all seemed to come at once, Paul raised his hand and said that he already had the team working on answers and that he would be talking with Susan Renly right after the meeting.

"I'm happy to change my schedule to make tomorrow's meeting," Tim volunteered. "But I'm not sure Stephanie will be happy to have me there. Anyway, there's not a whole lot we can do right now about JCN's latest stunt, and we need to get back to the purpose of this meeting."

With that, the group spent nearly two hours reviewing and finalizing the deal levers, prioritizing them, and establishing the limits for each. The result, shown in Table 2.2, was based on the AIC integration as well as consideration for future acquisitions. This was essentially the third option presented to MFS in the proposal presentation, with the services reduced to support just Worldwide and AIC as Bill Sellers had requested. The final deal would almost certainly differ based on the specific items negotiated, but Paul now had his marching orders for the negotiation as well as the leeway he would need to negotiate a deal without consulting with Agile stakeholders.

Final Great Deal for Agile and MFS

Priority	Levers	Limits
1.	Dataccess Discount	30%–35% WFSI Only / 40% AIC / 45% Future
2.	Implementation / Services	$1.06M–$985K / $590K–$480K Ongoing
3.	Training 13 MFS Staff	$112K Onsite – $72K Offsite
4.	Close Date / Kickoff Date	2 Weeks – 4 Weeks / No Board Deadline
5.	Platinum Support	$250K–$220K or $125K/Gold Level
6.	Payment Terms	Up front – ½ Up front / ½ Completion – 3 Equal for 3 Years
7.	Case Study and References	2 CS, 6 Referrals, 4 Papers – 1 CS, 4 Referrals, 2 Papers
8.	CVR with SVP and CIO	Quarterly – Semiannually
9.	Pricing Guarantee	3 Years – 3 Years with Option to Extend 1 Year

Agile

Table 2.2

Paul was pleased with what the group had accomplished. But his concern was growing that there might be more to the latest JCN offer than anyone had considered. After all, they were certainly not going down without a fight. A well-capitalized company, deeply entrenched in their space, JCN would likely take an initial, even substantial, loss to protect their territory. Setting that aside for the moment, the team's list of deal levers and limits was finally complete.

Here's what a great deal might look like to Agile.

1. **Software and Storage:** Dataccess software and storage for Worldwide alone (list price $20 million). Offer a 30 percent discount but go as high as 35 percent. Should AIC be included (list price $24 million), the discount may go up to 40 percent off. If the scope also includes future acquisitions (estimated minimum $28 million list), the discount may rise to 45 percent.

2. **Implementation Services:** Implementation services to meet the aggressive schedule

(especially with AIC included) will require a lot of top talent at Agile. Doug Hand, the lead engineer for services and support, wants $1.06 million and is unwilling to drop the price below $985,000 unless the timeline is also changed. Should MFS desire ongoing support of three Agile engineers on staff, that will add $590,000, which can be reduced to $480,000.

3. **Training:** Experience has taught Agile that customers are happier with solutions when their staff are fully trained on the software, and that training is more effective and better attended when conducted at the customer's location. Therefore, the cost for training fourteen MFS IT staff onsite will be $112,000. Paul is authorized to go down to $72,000, but only if the training occurs at Agile facilities.

4. **Close Date:** Normally the close date (especially before the end of the quarter) is important to Agile. However, this has been a very strong quarter to date, and Tim Rosser

and Jared Carlisle are fine with the deal closing next quarter. They don't want to put Paul in a position where time is his greatest weakness in the negotiation. That should be exclusively Stephanie's issue. However, if the close date goes past four weeks, then Agile will not commit to meeting the MFS board's deadline.

5. **Support (post-sale):** Agile has also learned that support after the sale is key to customer satisfaction. Paul will offer the Platinum Support level with a dedicated call-in number and team for $240,000 per year, but if he is pressed on price, he can go down to $220,000. He may also downgrade them to Gold Support for $125,000 per year.

6. **Payment Terms:** Payment terms are standard in the industry. There was a time when up-front payment was critical to Agile, but now that the business has grown, it is less important. Paul will ask for up-front payment, but with implementation services included

in the deal, he is authorized to accept one half payment up front, with the final half upon completion. If a three-year deal is struck, he can accept three equal payments for Dataccess beginning now and at each anniversary of the close.

7. **References:** Everyone agrees that MFS would be an extremely valuable reference account. Paul will ask for two formal case studies (Worldwide and AIC integrations) with references for six prospects and four conference papers; but Agile is prepared to accept one formal case study, four prospect references, and two conference papers.

8. **Value Reviews:** Customer value reviews (CVRs) have proven essential for both staying relevant to current senior management at customer accounts and positioning new opportunities. Paul will ask for a CVR every quarter with the SVP of operations and the new CIO, but he can accept a CVR twice a year.

9. **"Gray Year"**: If MFS really wants the more flexible arrangement that will encompass Worldwide, AIC, and future acquisitions as well as a three-year term, then Paul is also authorized to include a single "gray year" of pricing guarantees (for a total of a four-year price lock).

The meeting was adjourned so that Paul could get on the phone with Susan Renly. He and Tim agreed to meet again at the end of the day to discuss what Paul had learned and to plan their negotiation strategy for tomorrow's meeting with Stephanie Holder, MFS's senior procurement manager. Tim gave Paul a few pointers for his call with Susan. Finally, back in his office and already weary from what felt like a full day's work, Paul called Susan. She picked up on the first ring.

"Susan, I'm sorry it's taken this long to get back to you, especially considering the news about JCN," Paul began. "I've been tied up in meetings getting ready for tomorrow's negotiation with Stephanie."

"No apologies needed," Susan reassured Paul. "Given the news, I knew you'd get back to me as soon as you could. I got JCN's proposal first thing this morning from Bill Sellers' EA. Bill hasn't even seen it; he's been in meetings all day with some of the board members. However, Jack and Stephanie also got copies, and Jack is practically crowing about it. I told you that JCN would do almost anything to keep Agile out of this account," she added with mock scorn, "and now I'm sorry I was right. The question now is what we do about it, if anything."

Paul's day had been knife-edge busy, but he had given a lot of thought to JCN's new ploy, and he responded quickly, "You were right, Susan, and I guess it was wishful thinking on my part, but I was not expecting this move from JCN. In spite of that, Agile's position, for now anyway, is that this is just another bump in the road. We plan to go ahead with our scheduled negotiation with Stephanie tomorrow. If you think about it, JCN is still trying to make this about price, and we're not going to play that game. We still believe this is really about time and meeting the board's schedule."

"That said," he added slowly, his tone now solicitous, "since you've seen the revised JCN proposal, are there any other ideas we should be thinking about?"

"I do have a thought," she replied. "As I mentioned, Bill has been in a meeting this morning with some of the board members. You may recall that my old boss, Kenneth Beckley, was recently appointed to the board at MFS. It just so happens that Kenneth has been talking up the Worldwide mobile applications, portal, and website with other board members. He feels strongly that our current portal and mobile applications should be rebranded as MFS and become the standard at MFS. And apparently he has been quite persuasive! A number of them, including the CEO, asked to see a demonstration this morning, and that's where Bill has been!"

"How'd it go?" Paul asked guardedly.

"Well...," Susan chimed, inflecting the word for maximum impact, "Kenneth called me just a few minutes ago, and he said that the board members and CEO were truly impressed with Worldwide's technology and customer interfaces. They came away convinced that this is exactly what MFS needs to regain its competitive footing. He also said that Bill Sellers was very pleased with the demonstration and told Kenneth he was glad that the steering committee had chosen Agile."

"I thought you might find this useful," she added playfully.

Paul could feel his energy returning as he absorbed this news. "So, what I heard you say is that Bill, the CEO, and a number of the board are sold on the Worldwide technology we have developed jointly. Or do I have happy ears?"

Susan laughed out loud. "I think you've got it right, and I hope this is something you can use for your negotiation! I know you're under a lot of pressure as we've all got a lot riding on this deal, but I'm confident that you and Agile can make it happen."

"Wow, I can't thank you enough for this—and all your support," Paul gushed. "Tim and I meet later today to finalize our strategy for the negotiation with Stephanie, and I know he'll be pleased when he hears this. I'll let you know how it goes after our meeting tomorrow."

"Maybe that's not such a good idea," Susan replied, her tone again serious. "I've been told that Stephanie will tell you not to contact anyone else at MFS while you are negotiating with her, and I certainly don't want to rock the boat around here while I learn to navigate the channels. That said, I've seen how Agile conducts negotiations, and I'm sure you can handle the situation."

"Believe me, we do not underestimate Stephanie or JCN," Paul countered, "and we'll be ready for tomorrow. Susan, thanks again. I'm confident we'll be talking about the formal kickoff in a few days!"

By bent of training, Paul sounded more confident than he felt. While the board's positive reaction to Worldwide's customer portal and mobile solutions may have been the makings of a counterpunch to

JCN's proposal, the upshot of JCN's tactic was a bigger message: we're not going anywhere quietly. Now Paul and the Agile team needed to look beyond the news of the day and try to anticipate what might come next.

CHAPTER 3

Negotiating the "Right Way"

ALWAYS KEEP IT ABOUT THE OUTCOMES

A lot of my clients do a good job selling to outcomes and positioning value, but when they get to the formal negotiation stage of the sales cycle, they often let all the value they have worked so hard to create slip away. The formal negotiation is one of those inflection points in a business relationship where either all the good things you've done can pay big dividends, or all the "sins" you've committed will have to be atoned for.

As you advance in your sales career, odds are you will be selling to larger and more sophisticated customers. And it's a pretty good bet those customers will have developed fairly rigorous buying processes. Some might even call them machines, ones designed to make sales reps work hard for the business and negotiate hard for acceptable deals. Invariably, one of the final "cogs" in the customer's buying machine will be putting the sales rep in front of procurement.

How you manage the negotiation with procurement will have a big influence on how the customer feels about the deal they make with you. Are they dealing with someone they can trust and would want to work with in the future? Are they comfortable that they are buying the right solution(s)? Is your company one they can do business with long-term? These questions are often answered in the customer's mind at the point in the sale where they perceive both parties are in the "negotiation."[7] How do you ensure you are both addressing these concerns for the

---

7   As we've discussed, you've actually been negotiating from
    the very beginning of the sale.

customer and, more importantly, keeping the value in the deal by negotiating the *right way*?

Simply put, don't give anything away without also getting something in return by trading. When you trade items in or out of the deal in return for giving something to your customer, you are signaling that your *original offer* was valuable. You are more than willing to change the deal by exchanging value, but you are not willing to simply give it away.

Let's turn to the very simple but powerful rules for negotiating the *right way*.

OUTCOME-BASED NEGOTIATIONS THE *RIGHT WAY*

> **!** Do not allow the other side to **Anchor** the Negotiation on a single issue or Deal Lever

- Always bring the conversation back to the Customer's desired **Outcomes** and the "bundle" of **Deal Levers** to support those Outcomes
- *Do not ever concede on a single Deal Lever, but rather **Trade** for Deal Levers you want, or trade Deal Levers out of the Deal*
- Remember that **nothing is agreed to** or "off the table" until everything in the deal is agreed to

Figure 3.1

WARNING: ANCHORS AHEAD!

As Figure 3.1 warns, you should *never allow the other side to anchor you and the negotiation on a single item or deal lever.* There are two important components of this warning. Let's look at each separately.

The first thing you must guard against is letting the customer anchor you and the negotiation. This is how procurement (or any trained negotiator) will try to take charge of the deal narrative, and it will be their primary negotiation tactic. They want you to play their game and play it by their rules. Refer back to Chapter 2 for the discussion on how to manage anchors as well as how to effectively anchor the sale and negotiation.

The second part of the warning is equally important: never negotiate one item alone. Negotiating a single issue will quickly become a zero-sum game, where one side can only win if the other side loses. This approach to negotiating will ultimately damage the business relationship, and it usually results in *neither side* getting as good a deal! Always negotiate multiple items at one time. This gives you many more ways to put a deal together. While it may seem counterintuitive, it is easier to negotiate a deal with a dozen deal levers on the table than with just one or two. Not only are the potential outcomes mathematically much greater, you also avoid the single-issue, "distributive" (win-lose) form of negotiating.

BRING IT BACK TO CUSTOMER OUTCOMES

Always bring the conversation back to the customer's outcomes and the deal levers required to support those outcomes. This re-anchors the negotiation and, done consistently, will force the customer to negotiate against their own desired outcomes and, in effect, *negotiate against themselves*. They will come to realize that this is a bad idea—and not much fun!

NEVER CONCEDE—ALWAYS TRADE

The foundation of good negotiating is to never concede but always trade. In other words, never give up something unless you are getting something in return.

For example, your customer says, "We really want you to win the business; however, your competition is 20 percent cheaper, and in this tough economic climate we can't ignore such an attractive price. If you can match them, we can do the deal." What do you do? Concede and give them the discount? Odds are you have—at least once. And even if you didn't want to, your sales manager may have forced you to because they were desperate for the deal. (Not enough sales pipeline again!) In these cases, the logical question is, *Did you make your customer happy?*

Look at it from the customer's perspective. To a long-term customer, what message(s) do you send when you agree to drop the price? First, your customer just learned how easy it was to get a discount. Empty or not, their threat to give your business to a competitor won them an easy 20 percent price break. You gave it away just like that, and you can bet they're now kicking themselves for not asking for 30 percent! But their win will be tempered by the sudden suspicion that you have been lying to them, and all this time they've been overpaying for your products or services.

What just happened to your credibility? And from the customer's perspective, if you were lying about the price, what else have you been lying about? Now procurement will be wondering what other items they might be able to go after, and you are squarely in their crosshairs!

What's more, your customer is also thinking, *What's wrong with this picture?* Throughout the sales process and up to this point, you have repeatedly assured them that your company is the best supplier in the world, consistently ranked number one in your space. You have put together the best products and services to help them achieve their outcomes. If anything, you should be charging a premium. But you just gave away a huge sum of money at the mere threat of competitive undercutting. Naturally, your customer is now questioning whether your company and products are as good as you say they are. If you want to know how unhappy this makes them, you will learn—the next time you negotiate with them!

Let's review.

→ *Never negotiate a single deal lever (win-lose).* Rather, trade for one or more deal levers you want, or trade items out of the deal. Believe it or not, buyers tend to value these deals more. Why? Because they cost something, and it is human nature to value more the things that cost us more, whether money, time, or effort.

→ *Don't devalue your product or service by simply giving it away.* Trade for something of value to you and that costs your customer something. It is important to note that your customer will also value a deal more because you are trading and not conceding. This means that there is also more in the deal for them and that your original offer was always a good deal. You will move that value around via trading, but you will not simply give it away. This is the essence of saying "no" in a more polite and collaborative way.

NOTHING IS OFF THE TABLE

Finally, you must constantly remind the other side that *no single deal lever is final and agreed to until the whole deal is accepted.* Any resistance to this is another form of single-issue negotiation; deal levers that are taken off the table one-by-one will leave you with a diminishing list to work with. You must manage this with discipline because the other side will aggressively pursue closing out items and deal levers once they believe you have conceded something advantageous to them.

The easiest way to negotiate is on outcomes. Linking bundles of deal levers to customer outcomes takes away many of the tactics that procurement deploys against sellers. They will resist negotiating against themselves.

PROCUREMENT, PURCHASING, VENDOR MANAGEMENT, AND MYTHOLOGY

I have great respect for procurement professionals. Half my business is working with procurement management and buyers at every level, and I can assure you they have a tough job. However, there are certain aspects of their job and the approach that some take to their job that I do have a problem with.[8] To be fair, just as with many sales organizations, what buyers are being compensated or rewarded for is not always aligned with specific outcomes, business goals, and the ultimate strategy of their company.

My goal is always to seek and structure deals that are *great for both parties*, regardless of which side I may be consulting for. In my experience, when both seller and buyer try to do business deals this way, both end up more successful and ultimately make more money. This is a key component of a healthy, long-term business relationship built on mutual respect, trust, and delivery of value to each party.

But getting to this point often requires maneuvering through the procurement organization. So, let's

---

8 Perhaps I should do another book series targeted at professional buyers!

explore some of the myths surrounding procurement. Scratch that—let's *explode* them. I think you will find the truth to be enlightening.

MYTH #1
Procurement is the Center of Your Universe

First, I would like to set fire to the myth that procurement is the center of your sales universe. See if this sounds familiar: "From now on you will only be dealing with me. I will make the final decision, and if you try to go around me to close this business, I'll see to it that you never make a sale here again!"

Pretty scary, right? But let's look more closely at the assumptions of this warning.

Procurement is a pure cost center. The only reason they exist is to meet the needs of their internal customers, and any money they spend is provided by the business. When I make these points to buying teams, many laugh so hard they nearly fall out of their seats, thinking, *If salespeople only knew!* So, how can procurement be omnipotent? They aren't, and that is why their greatest fear is that you have done the hard work of *selling value to someone who matters*, tying their hands and ensuring that they have little to no power in the negotiation. They are not about to tell a senior executive they couldn't get a deal with you because you would not agree to an additional 5 percent discount.

But don't misunderstand. When procurement tells you not to go around them, they are not bluffing. So how do you manage that? When they ask you for a much lower price, you simply *trade key deal levers out of the deal* in exchange. The deal levers you trade out should have an adverse impact on the outcomes the key decision makers are trying to achieve, signaling procurement that you are happy to do a smaller deal, but *only if the key decision makers agree*.

After all, you fostered high-level buy-in and ownership when you presented options and invited the decision makers to help craft a deal that best helped them achieve the outcomes important to them, so it makes sense that procurement would seek approval for any changes that might negatively impact those outcomes. This is how you get the business back into the conversation without going around procurement. If they really want that discount—and you've done a good job setting up the right negotiation—they will have to ask for it internally!

MYTH #2
Procurement Is the Arbiter of What Is Fair

When procurement tells you they're only trying to do a "fair deal," what is fair, and who decides what it looks like? (They will say *they* decide, of course.) In many cultures (especially the US), fairness is often defined as an even (50/50) split when there is a difference— often phrased as "meeting in the middle." But in this context, it feels more like a weapon brandished to get you back on your heels. For example, procurement might strongly anchor on a 20 percent discount, then proclaim that they are being fair by accepting "only 10 percent."

The good news is that it's not your job to interpret what's fair, much less agree with the other side's approach to achieving it. If they want more or less of something, then *simply trade for more or less of something you want.* If procurement agrees to that, then you can assume it's a fair trade. If it wasn't, they would not do it.

MYTH #3
Procurement Knows What a Good Deal Looks Like

Procurement will also tell you it's their job to get a good deal for their company. But it's critical to remember two things here: 1) the goal is not a good deal but a *great deal*, and 2) procurement's only metric for "good" is often just price. I know this because most of my time with buying clients is *not* spent helping them become better negotiators; it is spent helping them determine what a great deal looks like *based on the outcomes* they want to achieve. And I can tell you that setting price aside as their negotiating "Swiss army knife" is like taking candy from a baby. So to be fair, procurement may know what a good deal looks like to *them*, but you can be sure that it will miss—by a wide arc—the target of a great deal for both parties.

Make no mistake, procurement will likely be prepared (often believably so) to tell you exactly what they want. But don't assume that this aligns with the results their business is trying to achieve. More often than not, what procurement wants more closely aligns with the metrics they're measured and rewarded by: once a supplier's bid is technically "good enough," then it is simply a matter of reaching a price or discount target. This is not a game you want to play, so you should be sure, early in the sales process, that you know the outcomes your customer wants to achieve, determine what a great deal looks like for them, *and educate them on the right deal levers to achieve it.* This sets up a common, outcome-based target and inoculates you from a price-only, "good deal" negotiation.

MYTH #4
Procurement Knows What the Lowest Price Is
Procurement obviously wants to ensure that their company is not paying too much for your products or services—that they're "getting the lowest price." But again, who defines that good price and who determines if they are paying too much (see sidebar)?

I'll never forget a session I held for the sales organization of a client in Las Vegas at their annual Sales Kickoff. Picture this: it was day three of a five-day conference. I was on the stage looking out at a rough collection of human beings. There were about 3,000 sales reps in the room and those who were not nodding off had roadmaps for eyes. They had obviously enjoyed the previous night's entertainment! I brought their chief purchasing officer (CPO) on stage and asked him a simple question: "How do you know you've gotten the best price from a supplier?"

Now we had their attention! Everyone (even those previously nodding off) sat forward in their chair and you could have heard that proverbial pin drop. After looking out at the crowd for a moment, the CPO said: "I don't know and I'll never know if I got the lowest price. The only thing I know is when the supplier tells me no." He went on to explain that if he still needed or wanted a better price or bigger discount, he would then ask the supplier, "What would you need from me to give me a better price or higher discount?" Then, as long as the overall deal worked for him, he was satisfied the company got a good price. This man understood negotiating.

There is no such thing as a best price or greatest discount. There is only *the cost to each side in terms of trades* in order to achieve a *better* price or *bigger* discount. You know that for every proposal you submit for the rest of your sales career, you will be told your price is too high, so why not be ready for it? Have the trades at hand and you'll close better deals and close them faster.

When you respond to *your price is too high* by stopping the conversation, running back to the mothership, and begging for a price reduction (that internal negotiation again!), you only empower procurement. Now they want to review your schedule, and it turns out your competitor is offering a much more aggressive timetable for implementation. Match it or lose the business. Here you go again—back to headquarters!

This is how negotiating becomes a "death of a thousand cuts." No single concession may hurt that much, but by the time the deal is complete, you're bleeding to death! Again, the biggest mistake you can make in negotiating is trading on a single issue at a time, conceding on each one of them, and allowing pro-curement to take each deal lever off the table after you concede. Remember, *everything in a bundled solution is related to everything else.* Be prepared to modify the offer (and the customer's desired outcomes), but never change one deal lever in isolation, including—and especially—price.

How prices and discounts are presented can have a significant influence on the subsequent negotiation of those items. For instance, too often we allow our customers to routinely anchor us with demands of additional discounts of 10 or 20 percent, or bemoan the constraints of a "budget" of only $500,000. If those numbers don't sound the least bit suspicious to you, they should.

Never offer a whole-number discount—and *never, ever* give your customer a discount divisible by five or ten. As soon as they see 40 percent or 25 percent, they will know that number is "made up," or at best a placeholder, and they will go after it with enthusiasm (especially procurement). Instead, offer a discount of, say, 38.6 percent or 23.7 percent. Give your customer a number that looks like some thought went into it, and let them know you had to fight hard for it!

The same goes for big, round-number prices for your solutions. How likely is it that your entire offer came to, say, an even $300,000? Instead, go with something like $316,483. The customer is more likely to believe that some thought and logic went into this price, and they will not go after it with nearly as much determination. These points are easy to implement right now—and be aware that the same rules apply to the other side. For example, a nice round budget number like $500,000 is almost certainly an anchor or placeholder, and you should treat it accordingly.

Finally, never fall into the trap of *defending* the value of your offer and the price associated with it. That is what procurement wants you to do. But at this point it's too late because you are speaking with someone who probably doesn't care, and if you have not already sold value to key decision makers, then you are at their mercy anyway. Doesn't it seem ridiculous that we give the customer license to lock in everything in the offer except price? This is how procurement has been trained to negotiate with you, and they do it because most of the time it works!

Hopefully, using the concepts above, it will no longer work with you.

Let's close with our Case Story to see how Paul and Agile prepare for and conduct the upcoming formal negotiation with Stephanie Holder at MFS.

CHAPTER 4

Case Story Conclusion

Late in the day, Paul met with Tim Rosser to finalize the plan for the MFS negotiation, which had been scheduled for 9:00 a.m. the next morning. He had spent the afternoon with the Agile account team developing the MFS customer success plan and preparing for the formal kickoff meeting that he hoped would happen in the next week or so. Paul was not superstitious, but he still hoped he wasn't jumping the gun on the preparations and jinxing the deal. After all, Agile had yet to formally win the business, and the negotiation with Stephanie Holder was shaping up to be a tough one.

Before stepping into Tim's office, Paul received a call from Caroline Borders, Agile's VP of Legal, telling him that the master contract terms and conditions had just been finalized and approved by MFS.

Good news! Paul thought. *One more hurdle cleared.* But he was still nervous as so much was riding on getting the MFS deal negotiated and closed.

* * *

"Good afternoon, or should I say good evening?" Paul remarked as he entered Tim's office. "I thought I'd start by briefing you on the latest with MFS before we get down to detailed planning for tomorrow."

Paul filled Tim in on the successful resolution of the legal issues as well as what he had learned from his call earlier in the day with Susan Renly. As he spoke, he thought he noticed a gleam in Tim's eye and a smile that grew bigger as Paul relayed his information.

Tim thought for a moment, then leaned forward and said, "Okay, I think this news is really good for us, but I don't expect Stephanie to acknowledge it. I wouldn't be surprised if she didn't even know about Bill Sellers' meeting and demonstration with the CEO and board members. Let's keep this one in our back pocket for now," he said with a smile. "Also, I think the power may have shifted in our favor in this negotiation, but again, Stephanie won't show it."

Looking directly at Paul, Tim went on. "I want to be clear on our roles tomorrow. This is *your* deal and *your* negotiation, and I will make that point to Stephanie. I meant what I said earlier today, that Stephanie may find she does not want me in the meeting. I spoke with our executive team about this, and they agree with my approach. They also agree that we will not let the end of the quarter put you in a bad negotiation position. I believe, and they agree, that time is really an issue for Bill Sellers and MFS. So, you are under no pressure whatsoever to close this deal early. I hope that's clear and helpful."

Paul simply nodded, but his stomach was doing flip-flops.

"How's that for a pep talk?" Tim quipped, adding, "I have every confidence that you can handle yourself with Stephanie, so don't expect me to take an active role or even be present for some of the conversations. Are you okay with this approach?"

"I think so," Paul replied, hoping he sounded more confident than he felt. "And I appreciate the confidence you're showing in me."

Tim laughed and replied, "You've earned it, Paul. We have a well-thought-out negotiation plan, and you understand the limits you're authorized to accept for each part of the deal. The only thing that's left is to consider the tactics MFS may use against us." Turning more serious he asked, "Now that you've had the afternoon to think about the upcoming negotiation, what do you expect from Stephanie tomorrow?"

Paul took a moment to gather his thoughts, then recited his list. "First I'm sure she'll tell us that we are not to speak with anyone else at MFS while negotiating with her. Second, she will bring up the revised proposal from JCN to shift the focus onto the price of our software and implementation support. Third, she will probably want to drill down on each line item of our offer and try to negotiate them one at a time. That's what I've got so far."

"I think that's pretty much what we can surmise at this point," Tim agreed. "So how do you intend to respond to each of these?"

"As for going around her, we will agree to that as a matter of course," Paul replied.

But before he could continue, Tim interrupted. "Yes, but we will agree to that *only if we believe that the outcomes Bill Sellers and the MFS executives are expecting are not being impacted*," he said, jabbing the air with his finger for emphasis. "If we do reach that point, we will make it clear that either Stephanie or someone from Agile must let Bill know that we are now impacting those outcomes, and we will need to know if Bill is okay with that. This is a critical point that you've got to make."

"Yes. That's our standard practice," Paul agreed.

"Good. And how do you think we should respond to the revised JCN offer?" Tim asked, heavily air-quoting *revised*.

"I will ignore it and not let Stephanie anchor the subsequent negotiation on JCN's pricing," Paul responded without hesitation.

"Right answer!" Tim exclaimed. "So, what do you see as the shortcomings and pitfalls of the new JCN offer, since we know they are desperate and still trying to make this a price-only discussion?"

Paul thought for a moment, then responded, "For starters, Bill Sellers will see this as an act of desperation and wonder why JCN didn't offer this approach the first time around. Second, JCN's offer substantially increases the risk that MFS will miss the board's go-live schedule, and it brings into question the ongoing reliable operation of the system. I mean, has anyone even heard of a JCN cloud-based offering before? Additionally, JCN does not know the Worldwide databases, applications, and interfaces like we do since we helped Worldwide develop and deploy them. *Finally*, rebranding Worldwide's technology as MFS would add a whole new level of risk for MFS—one I don't think Bill Sellers would accept."

"Whoa, catch your breath, man! Good answer." Tim laughed as Paul mock-mopped his brow. "And that is also why I believe we now have more leverage and power in this negotiation. Your answer also tells me that my confidence in you is not misplaced. Based on the work we did this morning and this conversation, I would say you are as prepared as you can be. Is there anything you think we're missing?"

"I can't think of anything," Paul said after some thought, "but I *still* expect some surprises. That seems to be how this deal has gone from the start."

"I agree," Tim said. "But I want to remind you that so far you've done a terrific job handling everything that's cropped up. We'll deal with new surprises as they come, so don't sweat it. Go home, get some rest, and I'll see you at MFS headquarters tomorrow morning around 8:45."

As Paul left Tim's office, he felt he was as prepared as could be expected, which gave him a much-needed boost of confidence. But he also knew this deal was far from won.

* * *

After what seemed like an endless series of long days and short nights, Paul was exhausted and anxious about the upcoming negotiation. This would be the biggest deal of his career, but he was satisfied that his team had done everything they could to prepare. Further bolstering his morale were the numerous (and humorous) texts from Jane, Doug, Jared, and even Caroline Borders, wishing him good luck and stating they had every confidence that he would land the MFS "whale."

All the team's hard work of the past weeks now came down to Paul's ability to negotiate a great deal with MFS, and he was feeling the pressure. While Tim Rosser would also be attending the meeting (at Stephanie Holder's request), Tim had made it clear that this was Paul's show—which of course only added to the pressure. Paul also had a nagging feeling that when Tim said "Stephanie may find she does not want me there," he had a surprise up his sleeve—and perhaps not a pleasant one.

After another fitful "pregame" night, marked more by sporadic napping than anything resembling sleep, Paul reviewed the negotiation plan one last time, promising himself he'd take a vacation—regardless of the outcome—once this MFS deal was over. The key would be keeping his cool and focusing the conversation on the outcomes and the bundled offers to produce those outcomes. He couldn't allow Stephanie to make the negotiation about price by anchoring the conversation around the latest JCN offer. But as he thought about it, he wondered if he couldn't use the AIC acquisition as a sweetener for both her and

JCN. Wouldn't this advance his strategy of making the negotiation about MFS's outcomes? It would all depend on whether Stephanie knew anything about the demonstration Bill Sellers had seen the day before, along with the board and the CEO.

Paul got an early start and arrived at MFS headquarters well ahead of schedule. For his part, Tim showed up fifteen minutes before the meeting, looking fresh and energized.

"I feel ready, but you *look* ready," Paul quipped at Tim. They laughed and shook hands, then Paul took the few minutes they had to brief Tim on his thinking about the AIC acquisition and the potential value of offering to trade that out of the deal and use it to set up a more outcome-based negotiation.

Tim reflected for a moment. "Good thinking!" he said. "That might be a smart move. But let's see how things go with Stephanie and I'll let you make the call. Remember, I'm only here because she demanded it. I have every confidence you will do a terrific job!"

At that moment, Stephanie stepped out of an elevator and approached Paul and Tim. They exchanged brief pleasantries and she motioned for them to follow her to a reserved conference room. The room was small, with a table, four chairs, a whiteboard, and no windows.

Looks more like the precinct than a conference room, Paul thought, taking in the Spartan setting.

Pulling two large files out of her case, Stephanie got right down to business. "Gentlemen, thank you for being on time for our meeting. I value promptness and we have a lot to cover! Before we begin, I want to set a few ground rules and update you on some significant changes since we last spoke on Friday. Sound good?"

Paul and Tim nodded. "Here we go," Paul mouthed silently as he and Tim glanced at each other.

"First, let's set the ground rules. As of right now, you are to speak with no one else at MFS until this negotiation is concluded. That should be perfectly clear, and I have already sent emails to MFS *and* Worldwide staff to that effect. Any questions?" she queried, arching her eyebrows.

"Perfectly clear," Paul echoed. "However, we do want to raise one exception."

Stephanie's brows now grew to peaks, as if to say *this better be good*.

Paul continued, "If at any point, we feel that what is being discussed and proposed here with you will in any way negatively impact the outcomes we have committed to delivering to MFS, then we will raise that issue. And we expect that Bill Sellers will be notified and agree to any changes before we can agree to them."

Stephanie visibly stiffened and cocked her head, as if both repulsed and confused. Looking first at Paul and then Tim, she declared, "No vendor has ever challenged this before, and I have to tell you, Paul, that you risk getting Agile off on the wrong foot in this negotiation. What I just stated is MFS corporate policy, and we don't put it out there as a point to be challenged."

But before Paul could respond, Tim jumped in. "Look, Stephanie, we agree to your policy and we don't see any reason to reach out to anyone at MFS during this negotiation. But as Paul said, if what you ask us to agree to will have a negative impact on the outcomes we've committed to—*especially the board deadline and timetable detailed in our proposal*—then we simply want Bill Sellers, as the ranking member of the steering committee, to agree to the new outcomes before we formally agree to them. We also ask that you take those changes to Bill. However, if for some reason any potential impacts are not brought to Bill's attention, then we reserve the right to inform him of those impacts in order to get his sign-off—or not. That's our corporate policy," he concluded, leaning on our with a gentle eyebrow inflection of his own.

This is not the start I was hoping for, Paul fretted.

Stephanie pursed her lips and stared at the table between them for a long moment, then responded curtly, "If you violate our corporate policy, then you must be prepared to accept the consequences." Her body language signaled that she was done with that point, and she moved on. "Secondly, after each meeting, I will send you a written email detailing everything we have agreed to. You will have until the beginning of the next business day to either refute or challenge what is in the email. Otherwise, it will be taken to fairly represent what we have agreed to at that point in time."

"Any questions?" she asked, again with the eyebrows!

"Yes, I do have two issues with what you just said," Paul began, finally joining Tim in the scrum. "First, we would like up to twenty-four hours to review and comment. That way, in case we receive your email late in the day, we'll have adequate time to read and respond. Second, we may be agreeing to what has been said in the meetings, but we will not agree to anything being settled and off the table in the negotiation until *all items* are agreed to."

Stephanie shifted her gaze to Tim and asked, "Do you agree with what Paul just said?"

Without hesitation, Tim responded calmly, "Yes, I do. Paul speaks for Agile, and rest assured he has the backing of me and our executive team. So, how are we doing with the ground rules? Are there any more or can we move on to working out a mutually beneficial deal?"

Paul and Tim were sticking to their script, but they were hardly winning any points with Stephanie, and Paul was beginning to wonder if this meeting would be over before they even had a chance to begin. But Stephanie forced a terse smile and said, "I think that pretty much covers it. So why don't we get to the real issue at hand."

Showtime! Paul thought.

"You may not be aware," she said expectantly, "but the situation here has changed significantly since last Friday when the steering committee selected Agile."

Paul and Tim waited silently for what they knew was coming, curious to hear the spin Stephanie would put on it.

"Since then," she continued, "we have received a revised proposal from JCN that puts things in an entirely different light. In fact, a few people on the committee think we should revisit the decision we made on Friday."

I bet those "few" people are you and Jack Grossman, Paul brooded. The knot in his stomach was tightening, but Tim sat with a calm smile.

"I think this revised proposal," she said, jabbing a stack of papers with her finger, "is very beneficial to MFS. The pricing is much lower. I would call it a significant fraction of your costs. *And* it addresses and *surpasses* anything you provided in your offering." She went on to extoll other virtues of JCN's proposal. "I'm sorry to spring this on you with no warning," she concluded flatly, "but if you were in our shoes, I'm sure you would be thinking the same thing. What do you think we should do about it?"

Tim pushed his chair back and stood up quickly, startling both Stephanie and Paul. "Let me be sure I heard you correctly," he said, firmly but calmly. "You just got a last-minute proposal from JCN, and you've determined that it is better and much cheaper than our offering. Does that sum it up?"

Stephanie nodded yes and Tim continued, pacing the small room, "Then if I were in your shoes, I would take their offer before they withdraw it. Don't waste another minute talking with us because there is no way Agile is going to come close to their pricing, nor do we intend to try. We'd just be wasting each other's time. I recommend we end this meeting now so that you can start negotiating with JCN."

The room fell silent, and Stephanie, clearly confused, looked from Tim to Paul. Paul, just as perplexed, looked from Stephanie to Tim. *This is not going the way I expected*, Paul inwardly groaned, doing his best to focus while Tim gathered up his belongings.

Tim directed his gaze at Stephanie. "Agile truly appreciates the opportunity to bid on this important initiative for MFS," he said, sounding sincere. "However, given the situation you've just brought to light, I am willing to formally pull our offer so that you can move ahead quickly with JCN. We believe time is of the essence in order to meet the board's deadline, and you'll need that time to finalize a deal with JCN. By the way, I didn't hear you mention it, but I certainly *hope* JCN has quoted a timeline that will meet or beat the commitment Agile made to MFS."

Turning to Paul, Tim said, "You are welcome to try and change her mind, and you know what you are authorized to commit to. But if you bring back anything that is out of our agreed limits, it will not be approved." He turned slightly so that Stephanie could not see his face and winked at Paul. "Please let me know by this afternoon if we should pull our offer, and I'll personally reach out to Bill Sellers to let him know why."

Tim extended his hand to Stephanie, which she haltingly shook. "Stephanie, thank you for your time and I wish you the very best of luck—no matter which way you decide to proceed." With that, he cast a brief smile and wave at Paul and left the room. For a long moment Paul and Stephanie sat silent, busying themselves with their paperwork. Paul now understood what Tim meant when he said, "Stephanie may not want me there." When he looked up, Stephanie was glaring at him.

"If I thought this was some sort of stunt you both planned, I would end this meeting right now!" she declared. "But by the look on your face, I'm pretty sure you did not know this was going to happen."

"No, ma'am," Paul nearly blurted. "Believe me, this is not how I envisioned this negotiation proceeding! And to tell the truth, I'm not sure where we go from here. I guess the two choices are to pull our offer, as Tim said, and finish the meeting now, or try and see if we can reach a mutually agreeable deal. Which way do you want to proceed?"

Stephanie reflected for a moment, her features softened a bit, then she replied, "Well, I've got a whole day open now, so we might as well see if we can use it productively. But first, clarify something for me. Are you really authorized to negotiate on Agile's behalf?"

"If I wasn't sure when I walked in here, I can tell you I'm pretty certain now," Paul exclaimed.

Stephanie chuckled and cracked half a smile. "You know, what Tim did took a lot of guts. I'll have to remember that and not underestimate him in the future. I guess the same goes for you too!"

She's got a sense of humor, Paul thought. *Who knew?*

"Okay, so if—and it's a big if—we're going to do business with Agile, we've got to find a way to reduce your pricing. Are you ready to have that discussion?" she asked.

"Yes, I have some ideas about that and am ready when you are." Paul welcomed the more civil tone and what now felt like a more level playing field.

"Why don't you tell me what you're thinking and we'll go from there," she responded without hesitation.

Paul pulled out his file and glanced at a couple of pages, although he hardly needed to at this point, having memorized most of it. He just needed a moment to collect himself from the theatrics of the last few minutes, and he was frankly surprised that Stephanie hadn't ended the meeting.

"Well, as you remember," he began, "we presented MFS with several options. If we were to take out the AIC integration as well as any future integrations, that would reduce the overall cost by approximately $4.7 million. *And* it would allow you to award the AIC integration to JCN. If we look at this deal as more than either/or, it opens up the possibility of awarding business to both companies."

"That might be worth exploring," Stephanie said, genuinely surprised by the suggestion. "I don't think anyone has considered this approach."

Paul stepped up to the whiteboard and sketched out Option #1 from Agile's proposal. "Here's what I'm thinking, and 'I believe it offers several pros to MFS." He ticked the line items off as he spoke. "You have a long-term relationship with JCN, and this allows you to retain at least some of that relationship. It also saves you money based on JCN's aggressive pricing. It may even speed up the timeline since JCN knows the current AIC data, applications, and infrastructure better than we do."

Stephanie was fully engaged and simply nodded in the affirmative. Now Paul had something to work with. Option #1 was genuine, and Paul was fully prepared to go with it should MFS choose it. After all, as Paul had emphasized with his sales team, none of the options they created could be losers designed to force MFS to choose one more desirable for Agile, as that red herring would almost certainly be the one chosen. The point was to get the business, even if that meant sharing some of it with a direct competitor. That said, there were two other options to consider, and now, having finally captured Stephanie's full attention, Paul swallowed hard as his next move was potentially very risky.

"But there's one big potential land mine," he continued, pausing briefly to read his co-negotiator.

"I'm listening," Stephanie said neutrally.

"Are you aware of yesterday's demonstration?" he asked. "The one attended by MFS board members, your CEO, and Bill Sellers?"

"I may have heard about it," she replied with a wry smile. "Why don't you break it down for me."

Paul went on to detail the demonstration of the Worldwide applications, website, and mobile app, and the stakeholders' reaction to the demonstration. He then laid out the potential implications should MFS convert their entire go-to-market strategy to rebranding and utilizing the Worldwide apps and interfaces. For their part, JCN would have a steep learning curve just to convert the AIC data to the correct format. What's more, if they were to also tackle converting all MFS systems over to the Worldwide technology, they would seriously risk missing the board's deadline—while potentially incurring significant cost overruns.

"I know this may sound self-serving to Agile," Paul continued, "but we anticipated this possibility, and both the cost and schedule are already built into our proposal.

We can do this because we are intimately familiar with Worldwide's technology through various acquisitions they've made that we assisted in. At the very least I wanted you to have the benefit of our thinking."

Stephanie stared at her papers and kneaded her forehead, taking in Paul's message. "I'd like to take a break and talk to a few of our people if you don't mind," she finally replied. "Let's plan on meeting back here in two hours. Is that okay with you?" Paul agreed and she quickly scooped up her papers and left.

Paul headed for a coffee shop close by where he could fortify with caffeine. He found a quiet table alone in the corner and called Tim Rosser.

"Do you still love me?" Tim answered.

Paul deadpanned, "Yes, but some days more than others!"

Tim laughed out loud and asked how the negotiation was going. Paul filled him in on the latest, including his suspicion that Stephanie had not been aware of yesterday's demonstration, and she was now buying time to fact-check.

"That demonstration was a great call on your part!" Tim exclaimed. "I think it will significantly change the dynamics of this negotiation. Like I said before, it has given us much more leverage due to the political angle, and it really highlighted the increased risk if they go with JCN. Be sure to loop me in on any new developments, and let's plan on talking when you two finish for the day."

"So why didn't you at least let me in on your plan today?" Paul pressed.

"That would have killed any element of surprise," Tim explained, "and I needed Stephanie to know you were not part of some posturing or stunt and that I meant it when I told her I had no intention of even trying to meet JCN's pricing. I wanted her to know that the power in this negotiation had shifted after the selection by the steering committee and that we knew it. I also wanted her to know that you were empowered to negotiate on our behalf. Sorry for springing the good cop role on you like that, but it looks like you pulled it off!"

"I guess we'll see," Paul chuckled. "But I look forward to *never* going through that again!"

They confirmed a meetup in Tim's office at the end of the day, and Paul mulled over what the rest of his meeting with Stephanie would bring.

* * *

Arriving fifteen minutes early to MFS headquarters, Paul was surprised to see Stephanie already sitting in the conference room. Curiously, the whiteboard where he had sketched out Option #1 had been wiped clean. Stephanie welcomed Paul with a slight smile.

Good start, Paul thought.

Then hesitantly she said, "Paul, I want to thank you for filling me in on the demonstration yesterday. From all accounts, it was pretty much as you described it." She shifted uncomfortably. "I'm going to do something I don't normally—well, ever—do. I'm going to trust you."

She went on to say that Option #1 was out and that MFS wanted to pursue Option #3, which included the AIC integration as well as potential future acquisitions, but MFS did not want to pay for any services for future acquisitions until those services were scoped and delivered.

Paul sat quietly and nodded. Somehow a celebratory fist pump seemed inappropriate under the circumstances.

"In addition, we want to get this deal signed as soon as possible," Stephanie continued. "I don't know how you did it, but my legal department tells me that we have a fully signed master contract with Agile, so the only thing left is for you and me to finalize the terms of this SOW. Are you up for having a working lunch and seeing if we can get this deal negotiated before the day is done?"

"I'm at your disposal for as long as it takes." Paul forced himself to sound calmer than he felt. Rationally, he shouldn't have been shocked at this moment, given the amount of work he and his team had done to prepare for this negotiation. Agile had skillfully sold value to the right people in the organization at the right time in the sales process, and then proven through successful testing and demonstration that they could save MFS a significant amount of time. This translated to a real competitive advantage, even against a competitor willing to severely discount their offering. All Stephanie had to do was validate all of this with the right stakeholders, and aside from some garden-variety pencil sharpening, there was little more she could do.

"Good!" she replied. "We're going to have to find some cost savings in your offer. Otherwise, I would not be doing my job."

For once, they laughed together.

"Okay, let's get started," Paul began. "I have some ideas where you can save money. Shall I put them on the whiteboard, and we can start from there?"

"That's as good a place as any," she agreed, moving her chair around to Paul's side of the table to better see the whiteboard. "Let's see what you have in mind."

Finally, we're having the right negotiation, Paul thought.

It was a long but productive day. As everyone had expected, Stephanie was a tough negotiator, but Paul was able to stick to his guns and trade for items important to Agile in the deal without giving anything away. For instance, in exchange for a three-year deal, Paul was able to give Stephanie an additional 4.3 percent in discount on software and storage, while locking in rates for any future acquisitions for an additional "gray" year after the three-year period. Stephanie agreed to MFS supporting a case study, speaking at a conference, and providing six references (assuming all went as planned) in exchange for a $60,000 reduction in implementation services.

Both agreed that training of MFS staff should occur at MFS facilities and that ongoing platinum-level support should not be changed. Payment terms for software and storage were set at three equal payments at the beginning of each contract year. However, Stephanie would not agree to pay for implementation services until the implementation was satisfactorily completed. Paul and his team had not anticipated this request, but he decided it was not unreasonable. Besides, with an expected timeline of only five weeks to complete the Worldwide integration, it would not delay billing by more than six weeks or so, at most. Since the cost of integration support was less than ten percent of the deal, Paul expected no issues from Agile finance. Likewise, the AIC integration services would be invoiced upon successful completion.

When Stephanie again pressed hard for an additional reduction in the cost of implementation services (beyond the $60,000 already given), Paul responded that there was no room to go any lower unless MFS was willing to both agree to the use of less experienced (and thus less costly) personnel from Agile and accept a much longer implementation timeline that could potentially threaten the board's deadline. Stephanie quickly replied that neither of those were acceptable to MFS, then promptly closed her notebook. With that, the formal negotiation was over.

All in all, Paul was happy with the deal he had negotiated; he had successfully worked the *deal levers* within the *limits* he had been given. Stephanie too seemed satisfied with the final arrangements as she told Paul that the agreement would be ready for signature the next day.

"So, are you authorized to sign the contract too?" she quipped with a smile.

"I am definitely *not* authorized to do that," Paul laughed. "But if MFS couriers it over, it will be signed by an Agile executive and in your hands no later than Thursday morning."

The last item was scheduling the formal kickoff meeting, and Stephanie asked how soon that could happen. Paul responded that he had his team working on the MFS customer success plan, which they would present at the kickoff. But to complete the plan they needed full access to both MFS and Worldwide staff to get their direct input. If everything went to schedule, the kickoff meeting could happen early the next week.

"Your team is free to contact anyone they need at MFS and Worldwide," she assured Paul. "I'll send out an email to that effect when I get back to the office. You should plan on having the kickoff meeting no later than Monday. Our senior management will make sure that you and your team have all the support they need to get the plan ready for the meeting—even if it means working over the weekend. Are you okay with that?"

Paul nodded and thanked her for her time and willingness to work with him. He added that Agile was very much looking forward to working with MFS.

"Do a good job and I'm sure we'll be seeing each other in the future," she laughed. "In fact, I don't usually attend this sort of thing, but I may just drop in on the kickoff meeting." Stephanie shook Paul's hand firmly and headed for the elevator.

As he left the building, all Paul could think about was the work he and the team had ahead of them to prepare for Monday's kickoff meeting. That and pulling off this integration ahead of the board's schedule, which would be no small feat and would require constant attention for the next several months. The thought made his head swim.

He was in the parking lot when it finally hit him: *Wow, he thought, I've just closed the biggest deal in Agile's history!* He needed to get back to Agile headquarters to brief Tim. It was late in the afternoon, but all he could think about was how much he was going to enjoy breaking the news to his team.

Summary

There's no question that negotiating in the B2B environment is complicated and growing more challenging by the day—especially if you keep negotiating the same way you always have. Simply walking into a negotiation with the expectation of having to give some things away is *not negotiating*. It is a form of charity with long-term negative consequences. If you sell to customer outcomes early in the sales cycle and educate the customer on what it will take to produce those outcomes, you will eventually be *negotiating the impacts to those outcomes*. Anything that changes in a deal will change those outcomes. This is what it means to have the right negotiation.

And remember, never negotiate a single issue (which is a win-lose conversation). Always keep the bundled offer on the table and agree to nothing—I mean nothing—until *all* is agreed to. Finally, don't concede on any one item, but rather trade for one or more things that are important to you, or trade deal levers out of the deal.[9] This is negotiating the *right way*, not least because it goes a long way toward confirming in the customer's mind that they are working with the *right company* and the *right sales rep*. Internally, your negotiation should be just as rigorous and disciplined as what you build into your sales rhythm with your customer.

But let's not forget, all your hard work can come to naught if your company is not prepared to deliver the promised value. Then, after the sale, you must get credit for delivering that value. *Only then* are you in the enviable position of having earned the right to ask for more business.

---

9   This is also an easier (and nicer) way to say no!

The final book in this series, *Can't-Lose Accounts*, will explore the management of the Value Lifecycle™ after the sale. How do you ensure you have delivered the promised value and get credit for it? From a corporate strategy perspective, how do you turn your company into a value management machine? How can management "change the conversation" from an internally-looking view to one of value—for both the company and its customers? I hope you'll stay with me on this journey!

My goal in writing this book is to help you to see that how you negotiate a deal (capture value) and the resulting deal itself are critical to your ability to actually deliver on the promised value. This is consistent with my observations, time and again, that salespeople who focus on value throughout their dealings with customers are the ones who have real job security! Remember, your goal is to not just win the deal, but rather to win a great deal, and grow the customer relationship!

As a final bonus for you, I have developed a companion online workshop to this book, also titled The Painless

Negotiation. It is available online at *mustwindeals* *.valuelifecycle.com*. If you're interested in working on a real negotiation by applying the concepts in these pages—something I highly recommend—please check it out. There are two tiers that include a stand-alone online workshop and a second version that also includes live one-on-one coaching from me on your negotiation plan. I am pleased to offer you a significant discount on either tier as a *thank-you* for buying this book. Just enter the promotion code "Book421" to get your discount—and thanks for being a customer!

How's that for value?

Good selling!

Made in the USA
Monee, IL
17 April 2022

94907214R00081